997

Cover *Survivors of* HMS Sir Galahad *come ashore at Bluff Cove.*

Frontispiece *The bleak Falklands landscape offers no shelter for prisoner or captors alike as British troops secure an Argentine prisoner of war.*

THE FALKLANDS CONFLICT

Valerie Adams

Wayland

The Arab-Israeli Issue
The Conflict in Afghanistan
The Division of Berlin
The Crisis in Central America
The Cuban Missile Crisis
The Falklands Conflict
The Hungarian Uprising
The Partition of India

The Irish Question
The Revolution in Iran
The Korean War
The Rise of Solidarity
The Crisis in South Afric
The Suez Crisis
The Vietnam War

Editor: Clare Chandler

First published in 1988 by
Wayland (Publishers) Ltd
61 Western Road, Hove
East Sussex BN3 1JD, England

British Library Cataloguing in Publication Data

Adams, Valerie
  The Falklands Conflict.—(Flashpoints)
  1. Falkland Islands—International status
  2. Great Britain—Foreign relations—
  Argentina.   3. Argentina—Foreign relations
  —Great Britain
  I. Title   II. Series
  341.4'2   JX4084.F3

  ISBN 1-85210-303-5

Typeset, printed and bound in Great Britain at The Bath Press, Avon

Contents

1
Operation Rosario

Port Stanley was the first settlement on the Falklands to be seized by Argentina and the last to be regained by Britain. The cathedral was declared a neutral zone where civilians could seek protection in the final battle.

Before dawn on Friday 2 April 1982, an Argentine fleet moved into position off the coast of the Falkland Islands. Commando frogmen came ashore in dinghies, and took control of the lighthouse marking the entrance to the harbour at Port Stanley, the capital. Behind them came 300 Argentine Marines who fanned out and captured the airport. More men came ashore in Stanley harbour, and others were landed by helicopter at sites around the town.

At about 6 am the fighting began; the Argentine Commandos attacked Moody Brook barracks, home to the British Royal Marines who provided the garrison for the islands, with gunfire and shells. They then joined other Argentine forces marching on the home of the Governor, Rex Hunt. He had been warned that the invasion fleet was on its way, and, with the officers commanding the Royal Marines,

had done what was possible to defend the islands. The British blocked the airfield and prepared to defend two beaches which they thought were likely landing points. High points around the town of Stanley were manned and the main headquarters of the British forces were set up at Government House.

There were, however, only sixty-seven British soldiers on the islands: by the time the fighting ended, shortly after 8.30 am, some 1,400 Argentine troops had come ashore, and more were being landed. Rex Hunt realised that further resistance was useless and ordered a surrender. There had been no British casualties among the troops or the islanders; at least two Argentine soldiers had been killed.

The Argentine flag was rapidly raised over Port Stanley, and the radio station and Cable and Wireless Office seized,

2 April: Argentine Marine Commandos raise their country's flag over the Falkland Islands, last governed by Argentina in 1833.

More than 6,000 Argentine soldiers were based around Port Stanley. The Panhard armoured cars were of little use over the rough Falklands terrain.

preventing communication with London. Rex Hunt was flown to Uruguay, and then back to the United Kingdom. The Royal Marines followed. An Argentine Army Officer, General Menendez, was appointed Governor of the islands. The Falklands, known to Argentina as Las Malvinas, and

their inhabitants had been declared to be Argentine.

The following day, South Georgia, another British dependency some 1,300 km south of the Falklands, was captured after two hours of fighting which left four Argentine soldiers dead and a British Marine badly injured.

The long dispute

The Argentine invasion of the Falkland Islands (known to the Argentines as Operation Rosario) followed over 150 years of disagreement between Britain and Argentina about the ownership of the islands. The Argentinians believed firmly that the Falklands belonged to Argentina but were seized illegally by Britain in 1833. The recovery of the islands was an important political issue for them.

The British regarded their 1833 seizure of the islands as valid because of an earlier claim, based on their discovery and on their occupation of them in the eighteenth century. Although there was not much public interest in the Falklands in Britain, there had been strong resistance in Parliament to proposals to change their status. At the heart of the dispute between the two countries was the issue of *sovereignty* – the right to exercise authority over a piece of territory.

The Falkland Islands lie in the South Atlantic off the coast of Argentina, 13,000 km from Britain.

The Falkland Islands lie in the South Atlantic, about 13,000 km from Britain. They consist of two large islands and a mass of smaller ones, with a total land area about the size of Wales or Massachusetts. They are bleak, barren and hilly. The population numbers about 1,800 people, mainly

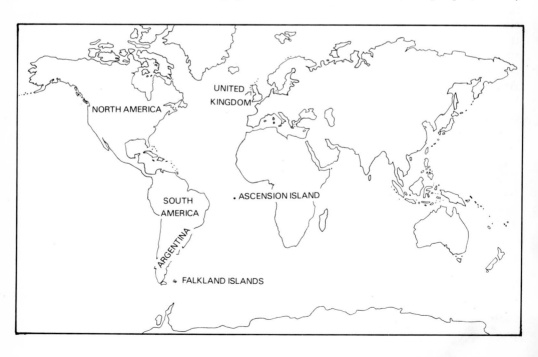

12

involved in sheep farming. In 1982, about 1,400 of the islanders had British nationality with a right of abode in Britain. The others were 'Citizens of British Dependent Territories' with no automatic right of residence in Britain.

There were no direct flights between Britain and the islands; flights between the Falklands and Argentina (about 640 km away) were provided by Argentina, with Britain providing sea transport. Since 1971, the residents of the Falklands had been eligible for a 'white card' which enabled them to travel freely in Argentina. In spite of these links with Argentina, the islanders wished to remain British.

South Georgia and the South Sandwich Islands are known as the Falkland Islands Dependencies. Argentina has claimed South Georgia since 1927 and the South Sandwich Islands since 1948.

Britain and Argentina had been negotiating over the Falkland Islands since 1965 when a United Nations resolution was passed requiring them to do so. Although there was some progress, the negotiations stumbled constantly over the issue of sovereignty. Argentina would not renounce its claim to the islands. Successive British Governments had promised, partly because of pressure in Parliament, to respect the wishes of the islanders. The most Britain would concede was that the issue of sovereignty should be 'frozen' (i.e. not negotiated) for thirty years. The Argentine Government did not accept this, nor did they agree that the islanders should have a right of veto over the negotiations. Argentina argued that the interests of the islanders should be taken into account rather than their wishes, and pointed to the extent of their dependence on Argentina.

In 1981, the Argentine Government became increasingly frustrated by the lack of progress in the negotiations. The islanders' position also hardened. The Falkland Islands Legislative Council refused to agree that sovereignty should be discussed at all in the negotiations. In December 1981, there was a new government in Argentina, led by General Galtieri. The new Junta increased the diplomatic pressure on Britain to negotiate about sovereignty, but also began to consider military action.

The South Georgia Incident
On 19 March 1982, Constantino Davidoff, a scrap metal merchant from Argentina, landed on South Georgia. His purpose ostensibly was to dismantle a disused whaling

station, a job for which he had received a contract in 1979. He had notified the British Embassy in Buenos Aires, the capital of Argentina, that he was taking a party of workmen to the island on an Argentine Navy support vessel, but did not await permission to do so. When the party landed it did not comply with the formal immigration rules and it raised the Argentine flag. The British Government protested to Argentina, but were assured that Davidoff had acted on his own responsibility, with no involvement by the Argentine Government. *HMS Endurance*, a British Royal Navy Arctic Survey vessel, sailed to South Georgia with a small force of Royal Marines aboard and took up position to observe events. The Argentine Government refused to make Davidoff leave South Georgia and instead called on the British Government to negotiate over sovereignty. Argentine naval personnel were sent to the island to protect the workmen. On 25 March, the Junta was – wrongly – informed that a British task force was on its way. They decided the following day to order the invasion of the Falklands and on 28 March the Argentine fleet sailed.

On 29 March, the British Prime Minister, Margaret Thatcher, and the Foreign Secretary, Lord Carrington, decided to send three nuclear-powered Royal Navy submarines to the South Atlantic, with the first one leaving immediately. The British remained uncertain right up until 2 April about Argentine intentions and continued to hope that the crisis could be averted by negotiation. On 1 April, they decided, however, to put troops on alert for deployment to the South Atlantic and early next day, shortly before the Argentine invasion of the Falklands, a British task force was ordered to prepare to sail.

Opposite *British soldiers lie face down in surrender, watched over by the victorious Argentinian troops.*

General Mario Menendez was sworn in as Governor of the Islands. He did not believe the British would succeed in recapturing Port Stanley.

2
The British Reaction

When the first news of the invasion came in Argentine announcements, the British Government was unable to check the facts as it could not communicate with the Falkland Islands. It was not until 4 pm on 2 April that a radio operator in Wales was able to get confirmation of the invasion from a radio ham in the Falklands. This initial lack of information paralysed government decision-making – but in any event the distances involved prevented any rapid military action.

On Saturday 3 April, the House of Commons met in an emergency session. Mrs Thatcher announced that the task force was being prepared with some ships already at sea. Her aim was 'to see the islands returned to British administration'. The debate was emotional and hostile to the Government.

The United Nations (UN)

The United Nations had already become involved. The Argentine Government had believed that its action would be greeted sympathetically in the UN, but on the evening of 1 April, the President of the Security Council called on *both* sides to exercise restraint. When the invasion was confirmed, the Security Council met again, to be presented with a British resolution calling for the withdrawal of Argentina's forces. During the next twenty-four hours, Sir Anthony Parsons, the British Ambassador at the UN, persuaded ten of the fifteen members of the Security Council to support the British proposal – enough for a binding resolution to be passed. On 3 April, Resolution 502 was passed calling on Argentina to withdraw her forces immediately, and instructing both Governments to seek 'a diplomatic solution to their differences and to respect fully the purposes and principles of the charter of the United Nations'. This reference to the charter was vital to Britain as it enabled the Government to cite the right of the islanders to 'self-determination', and the right of self-defence, as justification for the dispatch of the task force.

Operation Corporate

On Monday 5 April, the main task force, the aircraft carrier group, sailed from Portsmouth cheered on its way by large crowds. The carrier group was commanded by Rear Admiral Sandy Woodward, and included *HMS Invincible* and *HMS Hermes*, carrying Sea Harrier aeroplanes and Sea King helicopters. Its mission, the expulsion of the Argentines from the Falklands, was codenamed Operation Corporate. Servicemen and civilians had worked all round the clock throughout the previous days to transport fuel, stores and

The task force set sail on 5 April. The two aircraft carriers, Hermes (seen here) and Invincible, carried twenty vital Sea Harriers, as well as men of 3 Commando Brigade.

ammunition to the task force. The ships continued to be loaded by helicopter as they sailed through the English Channel and additional Sea Harriers flew to join the carriers, bringing the total number to twenty.

Over the following days, 3 Commando Brigade, the amphibious landing force, left Britain. The Brigade numbered about 3,500 men, and was commanded by Brigadier Julian Thompson. The ships which had sailed from Britain were to meet up with eighteen Royal Navy ships which had just been on exercise off Gibraltar. The rendezvous was to be at Ascension Island. This is an isolated island, formed of volcanic rock and lava, situated in mid-Atlantic, south of the equator. Ascension Island is a British base with an airfield, leased to the USA. It was the nearest secure base to the Falklands, although some African countries provided staging posts for aircraft.

Opposite *A Royal marine checks his personal kit before embarking.*

Below *Marines and sailors used the journey south to train, running fully laden along the ship's decks and firing their weapons over the sides.*

Operation Corporate required immense logistic back-up, much of it provided by the Royal Engineers. They built fuel supply tanks, laid a runway, cleared paths through minefields and dealt with unexploded bombs, mines and ammunition. Even for the toughest, war has its sentimental side.

At this stage, although Brigadier Thompson and his staff had been ordered to consider how they might land in the Falklands, it was not clear that the task force would actually go that far. Many people believed that the Government was mounting a show of strength in the hope of persuading Argentina to back down. It would take the leading surface ships of the task force about two weeks to get to the South Atlantic. This gave time for negotiations, and the key participants entered into a period of intense diplomatic activity. Britain began to seek further international condemnation of Argentina and support for its demand that the Argentines withdraw from the Falklands. The first priority was to obtain sanctions blocking commercial and economic activity with Argentina. West Germany and France had contracts to supply arms – ships in the first case and aircraft and missiles in the latter. Delivery of these was halted and on 9 April, the European Community (EC) approved economic sanctions against Argentina.

US involvement

Britain's closest ally, the United States, had been trying to improve its relations with Argentina. The US Government was concerned that if it supported Britain, its NATO ally, it might damage its standing in South America. In an attempt to avert conflict, the USA offered to act as mediator. Alexander Haig, the US Secretary of State took on the task personally. On 8 April, Haig arrived in London. He proposed that both sides should withdraw their forces, and that there should be an interim administration on the islands while a settlement was worked out for the longer term. The British insisted that the Argentine troops must be withdrawn from the Falklands and that they were prepared to use force, if necessary, to achieve that goal. With that in mind, the American mediators set off for Buenos Aires.

Initially the US insisted on an 'even-handed' approach. Smiles from Mrs Thatcher and Foreign Secretary Francis Pym (right) concealed suspicion about American intentions as US Secretary of State Alexander Haig (centre) sought to mediate.

3
The Retaking of South Georgia

Many Argentinians demonstrated in support of their Government's decision to invade the Falklands. The placard calls the British 'dirty pirates' – a popular theme in the Argentine press.

Haig's Shuttle

Alexander Haig arrived in Buenos Aires to witness huge demonstrations in the streets in support of the Argentine claim to 'Las Malvinas'.

The military leaders in Argentina had three demands: sanctions should be lifted, the British fleet should be stopped, and a specific date should be set for the completion of negotiations which would give Argentina sovereignty over the islands. They allowed for the possibility of an interim administration, but not for the removal of the Argentine flag from the Falklands.

On 12 April, the American team 'shuttled' back to London. They found little encouragement there. The British insisted on compliance with Resolution 502 – the withdrawal of Argentine forces. They would not agree to an early deadline on further negotiations, nor that Argentina should have an automatic right of access to the islands. They insisted on self-determination for the islanders.

15 April saw Haig back in Buenos Aires, after a brief trip to Washington for discussions with President Reagan. Haig threatened that unless Argentina met the terms of Resolution 502, the USA would move to support the British. He emphasized the strength of Britain's resolve and proposed a five point plan:

> both sides to withdraw their forces;
> joint Argentine/British/US administration until the end of 1982;
> the restoration of communications between the Falklands and Argentina;
> negotiations early in 1983 about the long-term future of the islands;
> consultations to ascertain the islanders' views.

The Junta were still not convinced of Britain's determination or of her ability to conduct a war so far from home and in the harsh South Atlantic winter. The Argentines did not reject Haig's plan, but neither did they accept it. Instead,

From London, Haig flew to Buenos Aires for talks with Galtieri and his colleagues in the Junta. They would not agree to return the Islands to their former status.

23

Opposite *Ascension Island played a key part in British plans. Royal marines from HMS Fearless used it to rehearse for the night-time landings at San Carlos.*

Below *Despite hopes of a diplomatic solution it became increasingly obvious that military action would be needed. Admiral Sir John Fieldhouse (third from left) had overall command of the operation. Major General Jeremy Moore (on his right) commanded the land forces.*

their Foreign Minister, Dr Costa Mendes, proposed a plan of his own – a shared administration with the sovereignty issue to be resolved at the UN by the end of 1982. These terms were sent back to London on the evening of 19 April: they were promptly rejected and the American mediators headed back to Washington, their mission unsuccessful.

Military Operations

On 12 April the British established a 320 km Maritime Exclusion Zone (MEZ) around the Falklands. This banned all Argentine naval vessels from entering waters within a circle drawn 320 km around the islands. Any ship entering the area, which was patrolled by a British nuclear-powered submarine, was under threat of attack.

By 16 April, the leading ships of the task force had arrived at Ascension Island. Communications staff, engineers and air traffic controllers had already been flown there. They were joined by planning and logistics staff, responsible for organising supplies of food, fuel, equipment and ammunition to the task force. Transport aircraft were used to fly these supplies to Ascension Island, where they were loaded on to merchant ships and taken south to be transferred to the task force. Other supplies were taken by air from Ascension Island and dropped to the task force by Hercules aircraft.

South Georgia

In great secrecy, the first steps towards recovering South Georgia had already been taken. Four ships left Ascension Island early in April carrying a force of Royal Marines and Special Forces. The Government had decided that South Georgia should be their first military objective. It was held by fewer Argentine forces than the Falklands; it was beyond the range of Argentine aircraft; and once captured it would offer a safe anchorage. There was a further consideration. The Government could not rely on public support for military operations lasting indefinitely. A quick victory in South Georgia would improve their standing while demonstrating the strength of British determination.

On 21 April the squadron of ships arrived off South Georgia. The weather was terrible, with heavy snow storms and rough seas. A party of SAS troops trained in mountain warfare went ashore by helicopter to reconnoitre the island for the main landing. The conditions were so bad that next day they asked to be taken off. Two of the helicopters sent to lift the men off crashed. Finally, a third pilot managed with great skill to bring his helicopter down and rescue the SAS

Below *The British forces recaptured South Georgia first as it was beyond the range of Argentine aircraft and would offer a safe anchorage.*

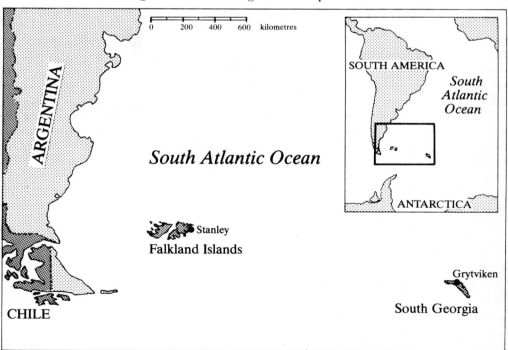

troops and the crews of the other helicopters.

On 23 April, there was another reconnaissance attempt with some forces landing by helicopter, and others going ashore in inflatable boats known as Geminis. This mission also failed, partly as a result of the Geminis' outboard engines failing, and again partly because of the atrocious weather conditions.

On the morning of 25 April, helicopters from *HMS Endurance* and *HMS Plymouth* spotted an Argentine submarine, the *Santa Fe*. They attacked and damaged the submarine severely. The British decided to press home the attack. The ships fired on Argentine positions ashore, and then a company of about seventy-five men landed by helicopter at Grytviken, the main Argentine base. They walked through an unmarked minefield to the buildings, where the Argentines surrendered to them.

In recapturing South Georgia with only one casualty (a badly injured Argentine sailor), the British achieved a major success in a politically acceptable way. The problems encountered were not publicized – it was several weeks before news of the near disaster leaked out. When the news of the success came out in London, Mrs Thatcher called out to journalists waiting at Downing Street, 'Rejoice, just rejoice!'

Above *The first British landing on South Georgia ended in near disaster when two helicopters crashed in 'white-out' conditions. A third took off safely. Three days later, the island was recaptured by the British.*

4
First Blood

As April drew to a close, the likelihood of fighting in the Falklands themselves increased. The task force assembled on 27 April as a 'battle group', with two frigates preparing to defend the aircraft carriers while the destroyers made ready to alert the task force to approaching enemy aircraft. The ships were stripped of highly inflammable comforts – soft furnishings and so on – in preparation for combat.

The British Government had already issued a warning to Argentina that if their warships or military aircraft threatened the task force they would be 'dealt with appropriately'. On 30 April, a Total Exclusion Zone (TEZ) came into force. This banned Argentine aircraft as well as ships from the 320 km zone around the islands.

The diplomatic war

In Britain, Francis Pym had taken over as Foreign Secretary. He went to Washington to discuss with Haig the possibility of a deal with Argentina. The USA put forward proposals which were broadly similar to their earlier package: joint withdrawal of forces; shared American-Argentine-British supervision of the local administration; and a plan for negotiations, lasting for up to five years.

The Organization of American States (OAS) met and considered an Argentine resolution calling for the withdrawal of British forces. Many members were sympathetic to Argentina, but the OAS failed to support the resolution and recommended that *both* sides should honour UN Resolution 502. Argentina then rejected Haig's latest proposals because they failed to meet Argentine demands over sovereignty and the length of the interim period.

On 30 April, the USA finally announced its support for Britain, imposing military and economic sanctions on Argentina. The Americans were already giving Britain military help in the form of fuel, ammunition and weapons. They

also provided intelligence information and assistance with military communications, including the use of satellite channels. The next day, Francis Pym was in New York for talks with the UN Secretary General, Perez de Cuellar, who began to work on ideas for a settlement. President Belaunde Terry of Peru also put forward proposals building on Haig's latest suggestions.

Francis Pym (left) flew to Washington to meet Haig. On his return he tried to persuade the British cabinet to accept Haig's proposal.

The Black Buck Raids

Below *The Sea Harrier aircraft played a vital part in Britain's campaign in the Falklands. It has a strike range of 470 km.*

The beginning of May saw the first real hostilities. At about 4 am on Sunday 1 May, an RAF Vulcan bomber from Ascension Island dropped twenty-one 1,000 lb bombs across the runway of the airfield at Stanley. This was in part a psychological warfare operation to demonstrate the military power and the resolve of the British. The runway was

not badly damaged and the Argentines repaired it and continued to use it.

The Vulcan raid, codenamed 'Black Buck', was followed by attacks by Sea Harrier aircraft from the task force, which was now stationed east of the islands. The warships also closed in to bombard Stanley airfield with their guns. Argentine Mirage aircraft flew out from the mainland and attacked the ships but without causing serious damage.

Below *A pall of black smoke rises from the airport at Port Stanley after its bombing by British aircraft.*

CAPACIDAD

Above *On 2 May,* HMS Conqueror *torpedoed the Argentine cruiser* General Belgrano. *The ship sank with the loss of 368 lives.*

Losses at sea

On 2 May occurred what became in Britain the most controversial episode of the campaign: the sinking of the Argentine cruiser *General Belgrano* by a submarine, *HMS Conqueror*. The debate covered various issues: who authorised the sinking; whether it was permitted under the Rules of Engagement which governed the conduct of operations; the location and destination of the *Belgrano* at the time; whether the sinking was a deliberate attempt to sabotage the Peruvian peace plan and escalate the level of the fighting; and, perhaps most importantly, whether there was a subsequent Government cover-up.

The *General Belgrano* was first spotted by *HMS Conqueror* on 1 May, although a ship accompanying it had already been detected. *HMS Conqueror* shadowed the *Belgrano* for some thirty hours, during which time it stayed outside the Total Exclusion Zone (TEZ). At about 9 am London time on 2 May, the *Belgrano* changed course away from the task force and towards Argentina. During that morning the Cabinet met and changed the Rules of Engagement to allow the *Conqueror* to fire on the *Belgrano* outside the TEZ. At 8 pm London time, the Argentine ship, which was about 56 km outside the TEZ, was hit by two out of three torpedoes fired from *HMS Conqueror*. It sank very rapidly with the loss of 368 lives.

The British Government has consistently claimed that the attack was necessary to save British lives. It has however been revealed that Government statements about the sinking were inaccurate in some respects – for instance, the time of the sighting of the *Belgrano* and the direction in which

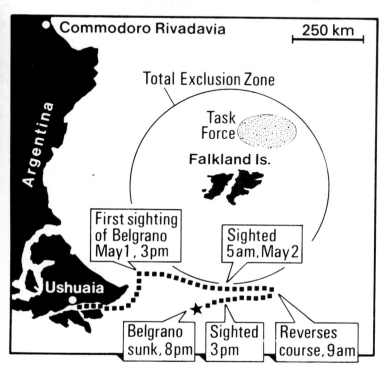

Left *The* Belgrano *was shadowed for many hours before being attacked and when hit, it was sailing away from the task force.*

Argentina soon took revenge. HMS Sheffield *had to be abandoned after being hit by an Exocet missile. Twenty men were killed. Fire and smoke hindered the rescue operation.*

it was sailing. The Government claimed that some details had been withheld for reasons of security. This argument continues to be challenged.

It is arguable how far the sinking was a deliberate escalation of the fighting. There had already been attacks on Argentine installations in the Falklands. Additionally, as the Government was quick to point out, Argentine aircraft had attacked British ships; had they been successful, the British might have suffered heavy losses. The fact remains, however, that the ship was sailing away from the task force.

As far as the Peruvian peace plan was concerned, Mrs Thatcher subsequently denied that the war cabinet knew about the plan when they decided on the attack. The news of the sinking apparently reached the Junta as they were considering Peru's proposals and on 3 May, General Galtieri rejected the peace plan. The sinking was bound to have

diplomatic repercussions; to accept the peace plan after it would have been unacceptable to Argentine public opinion. It is not clear, however, that the plan would in any event have provided a basis for negotiations acceptable to both sides.

Perhaps the most significant diplomatic reaction at the time came from Britain's allies. World opinion was hostile to the British action. Britain began to be seen as the more aggressive country. Then, on 4 May came bad news for the British: the sinking of *HMS Sheffield*.

The Argentine Naval Air Force had set out to avenge the *Belgrano:* an Exocet missile fired from a Super Etendard aircraft struck *HMS Sheffield*. Fires broke out on the ship as fuel burnt; thick smoke impeded rescue operations. When it became clear that attempts to fight the fire could not succeed, *Sheffield* was abandoned. Twenty-one men died and twenty-four more were injured, some seriously.

5
San Carlos

The collapse of the peace talks

On 5 May, the British Cabinet accepted the proposals made by President Belaunde Terry of Peru. They were formally rejected by Argentina at the UN the next day. The Secretary General again attempted to mediate. Argentina offered to drop its insistence on a fixed deadline for the transfer of sovereignty, but the British doubted the sincerity of this offer, especially since public opinion in Argentina clearly opposed any concessions.

By now, negotiations had continued unsuccessfully for a month. On 8 May, the British war cabinet decided to order 3 Commando Brigade to move south from Ascension Island where they were waiting. The men could not be kept indefinitely aboard ship and it was judged that any landing on the Falklands would have to take place by 22 May. If negotiations were going to succeed, it would have to be before then.

The British made a final offer through the Secretary General. They proposed the joint withdrawal of forces. The islands would have a UN administrator with three observers each from Britain and Argentina. Negotiations about the future of the islands, excluding South Georgia, were to be completed by the end of the year. By now, the Junta believed the British were playing for time. They rejected the British proposals, coming back with demands which would have denied Britain or the Falkland Islanders any part in the running of the islands. On 19 May, when the Government heard of the Argentine rejection, the task force commanders were given orders to go ahead with the landing on the Falklands. The next day, the Prime Minister told the House of Commons that all the concessions offered by the UK had been withdrawn.

Opposite *Argentine troops on the streets of Port Stanley: the fact that photographs and film were still being flown out of the Falklands showed that the blockade was not wholly effective.*

Above *Operation Sutton: the most dangerous part of the landing with men and landing craft exposed to enemy air attack.*

Operation Sutton

Special forces had landed secretly in the Falklands at the beginning of May to collect intelligence about the Argentine forces there. There were estimated to be over 10,000 Argentine troops on the islands. They were concentrated around Stanley and at a few outlying settlements. To minimize the danger to the landing force, the British commanders decided that the landing, codenamed Operation Sutton, should take place at San Carlos, an undefended beach on the opposite side of the islands from Stanley.

On the night of 20 May, diversionary attacks began at Darwin and other key places around the islands. At about 4 am the next morning, the main landing force began to go ashore at San Carlos and at dawn the Union Jack was raised over the settlement.

Bomb Alley

The loss of *HMS Sheffield* highlighted a major weakness of the task force – its lack of air cover. Harrier reinforcements arrived on 18 May, but the British aircraft were still greatly outnumbered. The Exocet missile posed a particularly serious threat. It could be launched from an aeroplane miles away, and then skim in low, making it difficult to detect. The ships could take various defensive measures such as confusing the missile's radar system or firing 'chaff' – strips of aluminium – to decoy the missile away. But they lacked early warning aircraft which could detect Argentine aircraft at a distance, giving more time for the task force to prepare its defences.

Below *Argentina had only five Super Etendard aircraft and five Exocet missiles. They were used to devastating effect against* HMS Sheffield *and the* Atlantic Conveyor.

Air operations presented problems for Argentina too. Their aircraft carried just enough fuel to attack the task force and return to Argentina. Flying low to evade the ships' defences used more fuel. Argentina had only received five of the Exocet missiles and the Super Etendard aircraft it had ordered from France. Most attacks were made by Skyhawk, Mirage and Pucara aircraft using bombs and rockets. The Harrier proved superior to these in air combat.

On that first day, naval and merchant ships lay at anchor in San Carlos Bay as men and equipment unloaded. Protection against air attack was provided by the ships' missile systems until the land forces could set up their Rapier anti-aircraft missiles. For over six hours, waves of Argentine aircraft attacked. The British replied with missiles, machine gun fire, tracer shells and flares. By the end of the day, *HMS Ardent* had been sunk, four other ships had been damaged, three helicopters and an RAF Harrier – one of the newly arrived reinforcements – had been lost. A number of Argentine aircraft had been shot down.

There was a brief respite the following day, but on 23 May the air attacks began again. At least six Argentine aircraft and possibly more were shot down by the British, but *HMS Antelope* was hit by a bomb which, although it failed to explode at the time, went off later, eventually causing the ship to sink. A Sea Harrier was lost when it crashed into the sea. On 24 May there were further attacks: two landing ships, the *Sir Galahad* and *Sir Lancelot* were hit by bombs which failed to explode (UXBs). The Rapier missile batteries were now in operation however, and had some success against the Argentine aircraft.

25 May is Argentina's National Day and the task force were alert for some special effort by the Argentines to mark the occasion. In a series of air attacks, *HMS Broadsword* was hit by a UXB. Then *HMS Coventry* and a merchant ship, the *Atlantic Conveyor* were hit, the latter by an Exocet. Both had to be abandoned. Still aboard the *Atlantic Conveyor* were thirteen helicopters, including three heavy-lift Chinook helicopters which were vital to the landing force's plans. Also aboard were all the tents for the soldiers ashore and much other equipment.

The stretch of water between East and West Falkland became known to the task force as 'Bomb Alley' as the attacks on the anchorage took a heavy toll of ships, aircraft and men.

Opposite HMS Antelope *was hit by a UXB – a bomb which failed to explode. When the bomb disposal experts tried to deal with it, the bomb exploded, killing two men.*

6
The Land Battle

For several days after the landing at San Carlos, the British forces consolidated their position ashore: landing supplies, setting up a logistics base and a hospital. However, after the losses at sea, the Government was impatient for a victory. Brigadier Thompson was ordered to send troops to attack the Argentine garrison at Goose Green.

Once ashore there was much to be done – defensive positions to be dug in, equipment sorted and, when possible, shelters put up. Behind the apparent chaos is an enormous amount of organization.

On 26 May, about three hundred men of the 2nd Battalion of the Parachute Regiment (known as 2 Para) began marching the 20 km to Goose Green. There are few roads in the Falklands; the ground is boggy and rough. This, together with the shortage of petrol, meant that the use of vehicles was severely restricted. Following the loss of the *Atlantic Conveyor*, there were insufficient helicopters to move all the troops, weapons and equipment. During the advance across East Falkland, the men had to walk, carrying not only their weapons, but all their equipment, rations, and ammunition – a load of 40 kg or more.

Very early on 28 May, the attack on Goose Green began. At first the battle went well for the British, but after daylight they were pinned down by heavy fire from the Argentinians. The Commanding Officer of 2 Para, Colonel H. Jones, was killed when he attacked a machine gun position. He was

Main Picture *23*
*May: HMS Antelope
sinks in San Carlos
water – the strait
between East and West
Falkland that came to
be known as 'Bomb
Alley'.*

Inset *This map
shows the two-pronged
assault by British
troops on East
Falkland which ended
with the capture of
Port Stanley.*

posthumously awarded the Victoria Cross. Finally, the British troops advanced on Darwin, the outpost of the garrison; nearly one hundred Argentinians were taken prisoner.

By the end of the day the main garrison was encircled, and the next morning the Argentinians surrendered. The British expected the garrison to consist of about eighty men, but found they had captured some 1,200 prisoners of war.

While the battle for Goose Green was being fought, the men of 3 Para and 45 Commando had set out towards Stanley. The conditions were appalling. The troops were continually soaked as they waded through bogs and streams and they had to sleep out in the freezing rain. There was no cover to conceal them from Argentine aircraft.

In fact, the Argentines did not expect the British forces to attack from that direction, nor did they believe the march possible. By 31 May, the British had captured Mount Kent, one of the highest of the ring of hills surrounding Stanley. By 4 June, they held the northern approach to the town.

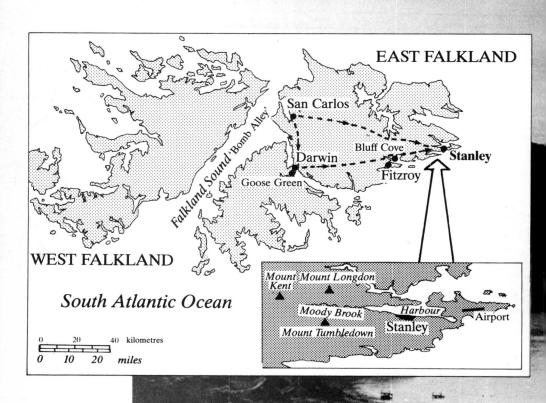

EAST FALKLAND

San Carlos

Bluff Cove

Darwin
Stanley

Goose Green
Fitzroy

Falkland Sound 'Bomb Alley'

WEST FALKLAND

South Atlantic Ocean

Mount Kent
Mount Longdon

Moody Brook
Harbour
Airport

Mount Tumbledown
Stanley

| 0 | 20 | 40 | kilometres |

| 0 | 10 | 20 | miles |

Air defence was the most urgent task facing British troops ashore. Blow-pipe surface-to-air missiles, like the one being fired here, brought down nine Argentine aircraft.

Prompt first aid, especially in pain relief and treatment for shock, administered by the soldiers in the field was the best way to save the lives of the injured.

Fitzroy

Some three weeks earlier, the liner Queen Elizabeth 2 (the QE2) had sailed south bringing reinforcements. Aboard was 5 Infantry Brigade – some 5,000 men from the Welsh Guards, Scots Guards and Ghurkas. At Ascension Island, they were joined by Major General Jeremy Moore who subsequently took over as Commander of the Land Forces in the Falklands. On 28 May, they transferred to smaller ships and arrived in the Falklands on 1 June.

The plan was for 5 Infantry Brigade to open up a southern line of approach to Stanley via Fitzroy. On 2 June, a small contingent of men flew by helicopter to Swan Inlet House, a few kilometres up the coast from Goose Green. From there they telephoned to Fitzroy where the Falkland Islanders told them, much to their surprise, that the Argentine forces had left. Part of 2 Para then moved rapidly forward by helicopter to occupy some high ground above the settlement. It was decided that the Guards should go forward by ship.

On 5 June, the Scots Guards arrived at Fitzroy. The next day the Welsh Guards set off from San Carlos aboard the *Sir Tristram* and *Sir Galahad*. The *Sir Tristram* arrived on 7 June and the troops disembarked, but the ship remained at anchor. Early next morning, the *Sir Galahad* arrived. The soldiers were still aboard the ship some five hours later when four Argentine aircraft bombed them. More than fifty men were killed and over forty injured.

UN Mediation

Throughout the latter part of May and early June, the focus of diplomatic activity lay in the United Nations. On 26 May, UN Resolution 505 was passed requiring the UN Secretary General to seek a settlement. This was followed by calls for Britain to show restraint – but in military terms, restraint was not possible without conceding at least part, if not all, of the islands to the Argentines. On 2 June, Argentina offered a major concession – withdrawal of Argentine troops to 240 km from the Falklands in return for UN trusteeship. In the Security Council, Spain and Panama proposed a resolution calling for an immediate ceasefire. Britain had, however, withdrawn its agreement to a UN administration, and vetoed the resolution.

Below *June 3 – At the United Nations, Argentina called for a ceasefire – vetoed by Britain and the United States, which later tried unsuccessfully to change its vote.*

50

The Battle for Stanley

Throughout early June, the British forces prepared to advance on Stanley. There were estimated to be about 8,400 Argentine soldiers guarding the approaches to the town. Generally, the Argentine soldiers were less well trained than the British. The leadership was poor, and so in consequence was morale among the conscripts. Nevertheless, they were well equipped and held strongly defended positions on the hills above Stanley. The hills also had minefields laid on them. The British lacked photographic intelligence and so had to build up their picture of the enemy's defences, including the location of the minefields, by a series of night patrols on foot.

Above *Casualties from* HMS Sheffield *are taken on board* HMS Hermes *by helicopter.*

Main picture *The face of defeat. Argentine troops line up, their weapons surrendered, the bodies of their dead piled unceremoniously.*

Inset *The battle over, the British advanced cautiously to the outskirts of Stanley. Only when the surrender was signed were they permitted to enter the town.*

On the night of 11 June, the British began their advance. They marched in single file along the paths they had previously marked through the minefields. They came under heavy fire but eventually overcame the outer ring of Argentine defences. The Argentine soldiers retreated or surrendered. The hardest battle was that fought by 3 Para for Mount Longdon. One of the casualties there was Sergeant Ian McKay who was awarded a posthumous Victoria Cross for his outstanding courage. By the next morning, the British had secured the outer ring of hills.

On 13 June, men from 5 Brigade moved forward to attack the inner ring of hills around Stanley. After a long and fierce battle, the Scots Guards captured Mount Tumbledown. Meanwhile, 2 Para had taken Wireless Ridge, overlooking the old Royal Marine barracks at Moody Brook. They then marched to the edge of Stanley, where they were ordered by the task force commanders to wait until there had been negotiations with the Argentines. Finally at 9 pm on the evening of 14 June, General Moore and General Menendez, the Argentine commander, signed the Argentine surrender document.

Opposite *There was no heroes' welcome for the returning Argentine prisoners-of-war. Later many were to feel neglected and cast aside by the country they had served.*

7
The Aftermath

The defeat in the Falklands proved to be the downfall of the Argentine military government. Thousands of young people were arrested during the Junta's campaign against terrorists and dissidents in the 1970's. Many disappeared. Now their mothers, known as 'the Mothers of the Plaza de Mayo' demanded that those responsible be brought to justice.

Argentina

At first, the Argentine Government refused to admit that the surrender had taken place. When the truth emerged, the Junta fell and on 17 June, Galtieri resigned. There followed two weeks of political in-fighting between senior officers before General Reynaldo Bignone took power on 1 July. The loss of the Falklands served as a powerful catalyst for change in Argentina; in October 1983, the country returned to democracy, electing to the presidency an outspoken critic of the Argentine invasion of the Falklands, Raùl Alfonsin.

President Alfonsin's criticism was directed at what he saw as an illegal act by an illegitimate government, but he believed strongly in the justice of Argentina's claim to the Falklands. Up to mid-1987 Argentina was still refusing to declare an end to the hostilities begun in 1982, or to renounce the use of force in the future.

The new democracy in Argentina was not free of troubles. Trials of the military personnel chiefly responsible for the internal repression and human rights violations of the previous years aroused intense bitterness and opposition among the military. This led to a military rebellion in 1987, resolved by the intervention of President Alfonsin and the promise of an amnesty for those army personnel involved.

Under President Alfonsin there were large cuts in the defence budget as part of a move to improve Argentina's shaky economic position. However, the Argentine Armed Forces steadily replaced equipment lost in the Falklands and modernized other items. The Navy acquired new submarines and destroyers, aircraft and more Exocet missiles. The Air Force increased the number of fighter/bombers and although the size of the Army was reduced, the formation of a helicopter-borne assault brigade was announced.

S.S. Canberra *and other task force ships returned home to an ecstatic welcome, complete with a victory parade through London.*

Britain

The task force returned home to an overwhelmingly enthusiastic reception. The British Government's political position was strengthened by its success and in a general election in June 1983, the Conservative Government led by Mrs Thatcher was returned to power with an increased majority. The Government's conduct of the campaign did not totally escape censure. Five years later, there continued to be criticism of the diplomatic failure preceding the Argentine invasion, and controversy over the *General Belgrano*.

It became clear also that the success of Operation Corporate had never been assured. The task force had insufficient air cover, it was at risk of submarine attack and it was operating at the end of an extremely long 'line of communication'. Had the Argentine aircraft attacked the supply ships and transports in San Carlos water instead of going for the frigates and destroyers, not only would the number of casualties have been higher, but the loss of rations and ammunition could have led to British failure. As a result of the campaign, the Government made improvements in a range of military hardware from soldiers' boots to shipboard fire-fighting equipment and electronic warfare systems.

For the British servicemen who had taken part in Operation Corporate, the return home was joyful, tempered only by regret for the lives lost.

The Falkland Islands

Perhaps a more serious long-term consequence of the events of 1982 is the commitment to continue to defend the Falklands. Since then the garrison on the islands has been maintained at a much higher level than previously. This is expensive not only financially but in terms of manpower and equipment which would normally be deployed in Europe and the North Atlantic as part of Britain's commitment to NATO. In order to reduce the garrison in the Falklands, and to allow its rapid reinforcement in the event of renewed Argentine hostilities, the Government decided to construct a new airfield capable of taking wide-bodied jets. This was completed in 1986, and the garrison subsequently moved into new accommodation at the same site. This allowed some reduction in the number of men stationed in the Falklands – but it will still remain very much higher than the forty-two marines thought to be enough prior to 1982.

The civilian administration of the islands was restored. The occupation of the islands, the fighting there and the subsequent stationing of large numbers of troops all disrupted the islanders' way of life. Perhaps the most tragic disruption resulted from the Argentine practice of sowing plastic anti-personnel mines indiscriminately, without recording their position. These mines cannot be safely detected and removed by normal methods and, after a number of British soldiers were seriously injured or killed, the mine clearance programme was put into abeyance until new methods could be developed.

The war has brought some benefits: new roads have been built; the Ministry of Defence has met part of the cost of a new hospital; instructors from the Services help in the schools; medical facilities have improved, as have mail and newspaper deliveries from the United Kingdom. Better communications with Britain go some way to make up for the loss of the facilities in Argentina.

A recent problem facing the islands has been the over-exploitation of its fisheries by foreign fishing vessels. This subject was due to be discussed in talks between Argentina and Britain in 1984, but the talks failed due to Argentina's insistence on discussing sovereignty. Britain then tried to reach a negotiated agreement with the Food and Agriculture Organization (FAO), the international body responsible for regulating fisheries, but failed to get an agreement in time for the 1987 fishing season. In 1987, Britain therefore

The Falkland islanders warmly welcomed their liberators – but the peace of the islands had been shattered.

unilaterally declared a fishery conservation area around the Falklands. Vessels wishing to fish had to obtain a licence and were then subject to limits on the size of their catch.

Costs

The cost to Britain of recapturing and defending the Falklands had amounted by 1987 to some £2.6 billion

[£2,600,000,000]. Operation Corporate and the replacement of equipment lost in the campaign cost over half of that sum and the new airfield and accommodation cost nearly £450 million. However, by 1987, the costs had declined substantially, and the annual running cost of maintaining the garrison was estimated to be about £100 million – a fraction of Britain's total defence budget of over £18 billion a year.

8
The Media War

One of the problems facing governments, military commanders and the media in any military conflict is just how much information to make available to the public. Information is so important to military commanders that they will risk lives to obtain it. It is equally vital not to have one's own plans, troop dispositions, and weaknesses revealed to an enemy.

Some of the media were accused of Jingoism – headlines like this went with invitations to buy Union Jack underwear.

63

That is the chief reason for secrecy in military matters. Other reasons relate to morale – that of the troops themselves, of their families at home who may be watching or reading about the campaign, and of the public. In this regard military attitudes to the media have been greatly influenced by the experience of the Americans in Vietnam. It is widely believed that the USA lost the Vietnam War because of the way the media portrayed it. The argument runs that because television brought the war in all its gory detail directly into people's homes night after night, public support for American involvement in the war was lost, despite the fact that on the ground the American forces were defeating the Viet Cong.

Set against that argument there is an important issue of principle. In democratic countries it is generally accepted that the electorate has a right to information about actions taken by or on behalf of the government. Without such information, the people cannot judge the government's performance, and so cannot fully exercise their democratic right to choose or reject a particular government.

Obviously there is tension between these two requirements – military secrecy and a public right to information. This is usually resolved by allowing that the public should only be denied information which, if published, would be damaging to security. This would include information which might lead to the loss of lives, or prevent the successful conduct of negotiations. Generally, the public recognizes the need for some degree of secrecy, and restrictions of this nature are broadly acceptable. The problem, however, lies in deciding precisely which information it would be damaging to publish.

Below *Opponents of the war believed that the media had failed to give them fair coverage – but critics of the media claimed that there should have been greater support for the task force.*

Left *John Nott, Defence Secretary, giving a press conference. His Department was accused of manipulating the news for political purposes.*

The Falklands Controversy

As the campaign developed it became clear that the Government was not prepared for the demands of the modern media for material and above all for pictures. At the same time, the media were criticized, on the grounds that they had given too much information away, and were unpatriotic.

The only way to get to the Falklands was courtesy of the Royal Navy – there were no commercial flights or sailings available to journalists who wanted to cover the conflict. At first, the Navy refused to take any journalists on their ships; eventually after intervention by the Prime Minister's office, they agreed to take twenty-nine reporters, technicians and cameramen. Apart from press statements by the Ministry of Defence in London, these were the only source of news from the Falklands. Their reports (called 'copy') were censored, either before being despatched from the task force or on arrival in London. Thus the Government had complete control over the information coming from the South Atlantic. Journalists and politicians claimed that the Government abused this control by concealing bad news, or carefully timing its release.

The correspondents found the Navy unhelpful. The

censorship was inconsistent – the task force correspondents would be refused permission to mention something, only to find it had been announced by the Government in London. They felt that they were denied information, and the opportunity to publish it. They in turn did not always appreciate the difficulties the Navy was facing. Perhaps the severest criticism of the Government was that it did not provide any means of getting photographs and news film back to Britain quickly.

Despite the restrictions on reporting, there was much criticism about the information being given out, and the way it was presented. It was argued that the enemy were being freely given information about numbers of men, equipment, and so on, and that speculation by 'armchair strategists' about operations was endangering people's lives. These commentators were retired Service officers, academics and journalists. Because of their knowledge of defence issues and their understanding of military capabilities, they were called on to analyse and explain events as they happened.

The second complaint was that the media did not present information in a way which, in the words of one MP, John Page, 'is likely to give due confidence to our friends overseas and support and encouragement to our Servicemen and their devoted families'. This followed a BBC broadcast which was widely, though wrongly, felt to have attempted to cast doubt on the British 'version of events'. The BBC was also criticised for showing Argentine news film and for reporting Argentine claims which subsequently proved to be false. The controversy was bitter, but it died down when an opinion poll showed that the public were largely satisfied with the way television was covering the conflict, and when the Prince of Wales came to the defence of the BBC.

A House of Commons Select Committee investigated the way that the media and public information had been handled during the campaign. They took evidence from correspondents, from the Ministry of Defence and from a number of task force commanders. In their report they discussed both the principles governing the release of information and the practical side of war reporting. Their conclusions, which defused the controversy, were that, although there had been shortcomings and failings on the Government's part, on the whole, the Government had won 'the information war'.

9
Past and Future

The battle for the Falkland Islands cost around 1000 lives, Argentine and British. It was fought because two states failed to find a way of settling their dispute peacefully. The reasons for that failure are complex; to blame it on such easy targets as Mrs Thatcher's forceful personality, or the Argentine concept of honour, is to ignore the serious and powerful forces that lead countries to act in particular ways.

The issue of who 'owns' the Falklands is a complicated matter of law, unlikely to be resolved easily. There are strengths and weaknesses in the arguments of both sides. Argentina claims that the Falklands are part of the territory it inherited from the former Spanish Empire in South America. It claims that the islands were illegally seized by the British in 1833, and it points to the fact that, geologically, the Falklands are part of the Argentine continental shelf. The question of 'Las Malvinas' continues to be of political importance for Argentina; it is a subject on which the country is united and on which people feel very strongly.

Right *Raùl Alfonsin was elected President of Argentina in October 1983. Although he criticized Galtieri's invasion of the Falklands, Alfonsin believes strongly in the justice of Argentina's claim to the islands and refuses to declare an end to hostilities.*

Britain claims that it has a right stemming from its original occupation of the islands. It never recognized the Spanish claim to the islands and nearly went to war with Spain over the issue. Its re-occupation in 1833 was peaceful: the Argentine garrison there at the time left without protest when asked to do so. The people of the islands have made clear their wish to remain a British colony and this, under the Charter of the United Nations, is a basic right – the right to self-determination. Finally, the British claim can be justified on a principle of international law, known as *uti possedetis juris* which, roughly speaking, means that the actual possession and use of territory confers rights on the possessor.

Argentina denies that the Falkland Islanders have the same right to self-determination as other colonial peoples because they are not the natural inhabitants of the territory, but are themselves colonizers. In the Argentine view, the islanders have no right to self-determination, so they argue that it would be enough to take into account the *interests* of the islanders, which would be best served if they were

Above *'Surrender is treason: sovereignty or death!': Angry Argentinians take to the streets in protest against the ceasefire. The issue of 'Las Malvinas' is a subject on which people still feel very strongly.*

69

Above *During
their occupation of the
islands, the Argentine
authorities painted
arrows on the road
indicating that
islanders, who
formerly drove on the
left, must now drive on
the right, as they do in
Argentina. They stood
as symbols of the
imposition of a foreign
culture.*

governed from the nearest country – Argentina. The
islanders themselves do not generally regard it as being in
their interests to be ruled by what is to them a foreign
country, with a different language and culture, and a regret-
table tendency to military coups and other forms of political
violence.

Britain has commited itself to act in accordance with the
wishes of the islanders, but that commitment cannot be
totally open-ended. It depends on the willingness of the
British people to finance the defence of the islands – something which has already cost well over £1 million for every
man, woman and child living there. It depends on the
availability of servicemen and equipment at a time when the
defence budget is being cut, and when there are claims that
the Armed Forces cannot manage to carry out all the tasks
laid on them. It depends also on the willingness of the British
people to see servicemen's lives put at risk.

In its efforts to force Argentina to withdraw from the
Falklands, the British Government claimed to have another
broader purpose. This was to demonstrate that aggression
does not pay. This is a fundamental tenet of British defence
policy which is based on the concept of 'deterrence' – of
making it clear to a potential enemy that aggression is not
worthwhile. In fact, the concessions offered by Britain
between 2 April and 20 May did represent potential gains for
Argentina, but these could have been justified as averting
all-out conflict.

Regardless of the validity of Argentina's claim to sovereignty, the invasion and occupation of the Falklands was much more difficult to justify in international law. International law is not like criminal law – there is no body comparable to the police to enforce it. There are United Nations forces, but they are limited in the roles they can take on. The British Government saw itself as putting right a wrong which the international community was powerless to redress.

Although the United Nations Security Council supported the British, the United Nations as a whole might not have done so. International relations are increasingly governed by the split between North and South – the international 'haves' and 'have nots' – and the Falklands might well have become another issue for North-South confrontation. Since 1982, the United Nations has moved steadily from support of Britain to criticism. The British Government has refused to negotiate with Argentina until that country declares an end to hostilities and renounces the use of force. President Alfonsin has not done this, and although there have been various meetings between the two sides they remain locked in stalemate. Unless that stalemate can be resolved, the risk of future conflict over the islands will remain high.

Below *251*
Argentine servicemen are buried here at Darwin. Altogether about a thousand men died in the battle for the Falklands.

Date chart

1592	Falklands first sighted by the English ship *Desire*.
1690	Crew of British ship, the *Welfare* make first recorded landing on Falklands.
1764	Settlement established on East Falkland in the name of King Louis XV of France.
1765	Commodore John Byron founds first settlement on Saunders Island, off West Falkland, in name of George III of Britain.
1767	France gives its claim to the Falklands to Spain.
1770	Spanish fleet orders British settlers to leave. Britain and Spain come close to war over the incident, until Spain returns the settlement, but without prejudice to the question of sovereignty.
1773	British settlement closes on grounds of cost.
1811	Spanish settlement withdrawn as Spanish Empire collapses.
1826	Louis Vernet appointed Governor of islands by the independent province of Buenos Aires.
1828	Vernet recalled after seizing three United States ships in a fishing dispute.
1831	USA destroys settlement in reprisal and declares the islands free of all government.
1833	Argentine garrison accedes to British request to leave the islands. British administration established.
1927	Argentina claims South Georgia.
1966	Negotiations between Argentina and Britain begin.
1976	Economic survey of the islands by Lord Shackleton.
1977	British submarine sent to Falklands because of fear of Argentine incursion.
1981	New Junta formed under leadership of General Galtieri. British Defence Review proposes withdrawal of *HMS Endurance* from the South Atlantic.

1982

26–27 Feb	Negotiations in New York between Britain and Argentina.
19 March	Davidoff lands on South Georgia.
29 March	Argentine fleet puts to sea.
1 April	Britain informs Security Council that invasion is imminent.
2 April	Argentina invades the Falkland Islands.
3 April	UN resolution 502 passed. South Georgia captured by Argentines. Emergency debate in British Parliament.
5 April	Task force begins to sail: first wave of ships all depart by 9 April.
7 April	Second Debate in British Parliament.
8 April	Haig 'peace shuttle' begins in Buenos Aires.
12 April	320 km Maritime Exclusion Zone takes effect.
14 April	Third Debate in British Parliament.
21 April	SAS land on South Georgia.
22 April	SAS lifted off South Georgia. Francis Pym in Washington for consultations.
25 April	British forces recapture South Georgia.
25–28 April	Meeting of Organization of American States.
29 April	Fourth Debate in British Parliament.
30 April	USA openly sides with Britain. Total Exclusion Zone imposed around Falklands. Task force arrives in vicinity of the islands.
1 May	British aircraft attack Stanley airfield. Argentines begin air attacks on task force.
2 May	*General Belgrano* sunk by *HMS Conqueror*.
4 May	*HMS Sheffield* sunk by Exocet missile.
8 May	Landing force ordered to sail south from Ascension Island.
12 May	*QE2* sails from Southampton.
14–15 May	SAS attack Pebble Island.
21 May	San Carlos landing begins. *HMS Ardent* sunk.
24 May	*HMS Antelope* sunk.
25 May	*HMS Coventry* and *Atlantic Conveyor* sunk.
28 May	2 Para win battle for Goose Green.
31 May	42 Commando occupy Mount Kent.
1 June	5 Infantry brigade arrive in the Falklands.
8 June	Bombing of *Sir Galahad* and *Sir Tristram*.
11 June	Battle for Stanley begins.
13 June	Inner ring of hills around Stanley captured.
14 June	Argentine surrender.

Glossary

Aircraft Carrier Large naval vessel with a deck big enough for aircraft to land and take off again. The British aircraft carriers are relatively small and can only take the Harrier 'jump jet'.

Amnesty A general pardon for offenders.

Amphibious Military forces used for operations launched from the sea against an enemy shore.

Charter of the UN Document which states the aims of the UN and the way in which they should be carried out.

Chinook Heavy-lift helicopter which can carry 80 men.

Commando Elite military forces trained for special missions.

Conscript Person who is enrolled for compulsory military service.

Deployment Redistribution of forces, usually in preparation for battle.

Destroyer A heavily armed naval ship which can be used in a number of roles – against surface ships or submarines, air defence, convoy protection.

Deterrence Seeking to persuade potential enemies that the costs of any aggression would far outweigh the gains, and that aggression is not therefore worthwhile.

Electronic Warfare The use of electronics in combat to disrupt the radars, communications, and other electronic equipment of the enemy. EW can be used in attack or in defence.

Escalation Increasing the level and intensity of a conflict, usually in the hope of persuading the other combatants to cease fighting.

Exocet A modern anti-ship missile which can be launched from a ship or aircraft, then skims the surface of the sea in order to escape detection by its target.

FAO Food and Agriculture Organization. An agency of the United Nations which coordinates international efforts to improve food production.

Frigate A relatively small naval vessel, usually equipped with guided missiles.

Harrier British aircraft capable of very short take-off and landing. Sea Harrier is deployed on aircraft carriers; the RAF has the Harrier GR3 ground attack aircraft.

Intelligence [i.e. military or defence] Information about another country, usually concerned with its military strength, the location of its armed forces and its plans.

Junta System of joint leadership, usually in military dictatorships, where several people participate on an equal basis in ruling.

Line of Communication The route along which military supplies and equipment must travel to reach a body of fighting men.

NATO North Atlantic Treaty Organisation. A defence alliance to which Britain belongs together with fifteen other European and North American countries.

Nuclear-powered submarine (SSN) A 'hunter-killer' submarine powered by a nuclear plant and used to track and destroy other submarines or ships. An SSN does *not* carry nuclear missiles.

Rules of Engagement Rules for military commanders governing the way they operate, and in particular setting out the circumstances in which they may open fire.

Sanctions Penalty imposed on a country, usually by blocking all dealings with it in a particular field – finance, trade, culture or military aid.

Security Council Fifteen members of the United Nations, of whom Britain, China, France, the Soviet Union and the United States have permanent seats on the Council. The Security Council is the body responsible for maintaining international peace.

Sovereignty A legal concept meaning that the person or state possessing it has the right to do as it likes with the territory it controls.

Special Forces Elite military units trained to operate behind enemy lines e.g. Special Air Service (SAS).

UN An organization founded after the Second World War to foster international peace and cooperation. Most countries of the world belong to it.

Viet Cong Member of the armed forces of the National Liberation Front of South Vietnam.

Yomp Royal Marine slang for a march, derived from a Norwegian word for cross-country ski-ing.

Further reading

Background

The Franks Report (*Falkland Islands Review: Report of a Committee of Privy Counsellors*). (HMSO, Cmnd 8787, London 1983)

The Falklands Islands and Dependencies (Central Office of Information, March 1982)

The Falkland Islands: The Facts (HMSO, London 1982)

Calvert, P. *The Falklands Crisis: The Rights and Wrongs* (Frances Pinter, 1982)

Latin America Bureau *Falklands? Malvina: Whose Crisis?* (London, 1982)

Detailed Accounts

Ethell, J. & Price, A. *Air War South Atlantic* (Sidgwick and Jackson, 1984)

Fox, R. *Eyewitness Falklands* (Methuen, 1982)

Gavshon, A. & Rice, D. *The Sinking of the Belgrano* (Secker and Warburg, 1984)

Hastings, M. & Jenkins, S. *The Battle for the Falklands* (Michael Joseph, 1983)

Thompson, J. *No Picnic* (Leo Cooper, 1985)

Windrow, M. Ed *Battle for the Falklands Vols 1–3;* (Osprey Publishing, 1982)

Argentine Accounts

Kon, Daniel *Los Chicos de la Guerra* [published in English] (New English Library, 1983)

The Media Aspects

Adams, V. *The Media and the Falklands Campaign* (Macmillan, 1986)

Harris, R. *Gotcha!* (Faber & Faber, 1983)

Index

Picture Acknowledgements

The publishers would like to thank the following for the loan of their photographs in this book: Camera Press 14, 30, 68; Express News and Features *frontispiece*, 10, 18, 38, 42, 45, 48, 52, 55, 60, 62; John Frost 63; Press Association *cover*; Topham Picture Library 8, 9, 15, 17, 19, 20, 21, 22, 23, 24, 25, 27, 29, 31, 32, 34, 37, 39, 46, 50, 51, 52, 54, 56, 58, 64, 65, 67, 69, 70, 71; Maps on pages 26 & 44 are by Malcolm S. Walker.